Using the EMPATHY DOLLS Approach

Developing emotional awareness in Early Years Settings

Published 2009 by A&C Black Publishers Limited
36 Soho Square, London W1D 3QY
www.acblack.com

ISBN 978-1-408114-47-6

Written by Kirstine Beeley
Edited by Judith Harries
Design by Bob Vickers

Thanks to the following for their input into this book:
Staff and children of Jolly Giraffes Nursery, Leeds
Staff and children of the Cleveland Unit, Middlesbrough
Lisa Clifford - Childminder (and children)
Laura Stanbra - Childminder (and children)
Anne Gallagher - Childminder (and children)
And everyone else whose commitment and enthusiasm for the Empathy Dolls Approach has ensured its success with their children.

Printed in Great Britain by Latimer Trend & Company Limited

A CIP record for this publication is available from the British Library.

Contents

About the author

My background as a teacher in primary, early years and special needs settings has meant that I have observed some really good practice when it comes to supporting children's emotional development and occasionally some not so good practice. These observations, coupled with years of working within the educational supplies industry (with short bouts of supply teaching thrown in for good measure) led me to a point where I saw the need for a tool to explore emotional development which particularly suited early years settings. I wanted to create an approach that would help to support **every** child and not just be used to highlight what I perceived as the big, headline-grabbing issues such as bullying, racism or discrimination.

I'm not saying we shouldn't address these really important issues. There are many tools and resources available that do this already. I just felt passionately that there needed to be an approach that specifically focused on emotional development and building a sense of self-worth for each child. I wondered if, by combining lots of examples of best practice from different settings, there would be a new way of working with dolls suitable for use in early years settings? Was it possible to develop something that acknowledged the emotional needs of even the very youngest of children in our care? The answer has been a resounding 'yes'!

Five years on and having delivered workshops to hundreds of early years professionals across the UK, my days are now filled with wonderful stories of the dolls' adventures. I hear of the diverse ways that the dolls are being used to help children acknowledge their uniqueness within supportive, emotion-rich early learning environments. Hardly a day goes by when I don't get an email or a letter from someone sharing yet another positive experience where they have been able to help the children in their care.

In this book I aim to highlight the principles behind the Empathy Dolls Approach whilst drawing on some of the array of research that exists surrounding children's emotional development, and in particular their ability to empathise with others. I have included accounts from many of the early years professionals who I have had the pleasure of working with and who have used the Empathy Dolls Approach to support children in a wide range of everyday situations. For their input I am forever grateful, their accounts fuel my conviction to continue to advocate this way of working and the principles behind it.

In writing this book I have tried to include as many stories and pictures as I can, but I would like to thank all of the early years and primary settings who have contacted me over the years with details of their experiences with the dolls. It is these stories that keep me enthused and drive me on to try and spread the word further about working with the Empathy Dolls Approach.

I cannot finish this brief foreword without acknowledging three people without whom this approach and this book would not exist. Firstly, my heartfelt and eternal thanks to Rosemary Moore, who introduced me, as a young, newly qualified teacher, to the joys and wonders of early years teaching. It is this commitment to individual learning potential that has stayed with me over the years and that forms the foundations of my belief in child-centred, play-based early years learning.

Secondly, thanks to my mother who having been widowed in her twenties, devoted every ounce of energy and love to bringing up my brother and me. She taught us to respect everyone as individuals and to look for the unique skills and talents that we all have to share with the world. All the more extraordinary as she had spina bifida and spent the best part of her life confined to a wheelchair.

And finally, my gorgeous son Luke, who has truly helped me to see the world through a child's eyes and whose enthusiasm for discovery and learning is forever infectious.

Introduction: Empathy and emotional development

'Empathy builds on self-awareness, the more open we are to our own emotions, the more skilled we will be in reading feelings.'

Goleman 1995

There are many definitions of empathy and over the years, psychologists, scientists and educationalists have all developed their own interpretation of what exactly it means. As Martin Hoffman points out these tend to fall into two generalised categories. The first where the description refers to the **actual experiencing of someone else's emotions**, as he puts it 'the cognitive awareness of another person's internal states, his thoughts, feelings, perceptions and intentions' (Hoffman 2000). The second definition focuses on **an individual's response to another person's situation** (vicarious affective response). This is the ability for someone to both feel and respond to the feelings or emotions of others. The use of the term empathy within the 'Empathy Dolls Approach' focuses on both of these definitions and hopefully provides scope for development of both skills, especially as it covers not only the children's own emotional development but the emotional awareness of the significant adults involved.

Although this approach aims to heighten children's empathy and emotional development we must acknowledge that research points towards humans as being born with a natural tendency towards empathic response to others in distress (Barnet et al 1990). Most parents or practitioners, experienced in working with toddlers, can probably relate at least one situation where they have observed their child showing natural empathy for another individual. As a mother, if you cry your child will start to cry. If you show anger, your child appears to have felt the anger themselves.

Researchers have observed many behaviours that suggest humans have natural empathy particularly in their earliest years (Coplan et al 2006) and now scientists have identified 'mirror neurons' which they believe are involved in the process of empathising (Carr et al 2003). It seems important to point out that the research shows that as well as reacting to an individual's own experiences, mirror neurons also react to the experiences of others and so form a physical part of the process of putting

From a very young age, humans both feel and respond to the feelings and emotions of others.

yourself into someone else's shoes and feeling the world from their perspective i.e. having empathy.

Hoffman points out that we have a natural instinct to copy or mimic the facial expression of someone displaying emotion, a skill which develops from a really early age with very young babies mimicking their parents' expressions. This in turn can lead to feeling the emotion related to the facial expression and hence feeling the emotions of the other individual. This automatic reaction would appear to build up our understanding and appreciation of the emotions and feelings of others as we grow.

It is also important to give children the opportunity to reflect on their own emotional responses to situations as Hoffman and others (Hinnant 2007) have identified the ability to be able to empathise by association i.e. by looking at a person's situation and remembering how you felt in a similar situation.

As I mentioned earlier one of the definitions of empathy focuses not only on the feeling of emotions but on the **ability to empathically respond to other's feelings about a situation**. The press has in recent years questioned whether the UK as a nation has lost the ability to empathise. In actual fact what they mean is have we lost the ability to react in response to feeling empathy in a way that will help to alleviate an individual's feelings of discomfort or pain?

In 2006 reports from Buckinghamshire (www.timesonline.co.uk) told of eight-year-old Cait Aitkins who, while crossing the road, was knocked down by a car, seriously injuring her leg. The press's outrage focused on the response of individuals passing Cait in the street. It was reported that at least six drivers drove by without stopping as she lay screaming in pain before someone actually stopped to help. As scientists have concluded that we are all to some extent 'hard-wired' to experience empathy the question in this instance is not 'Did they not feel what the little girl was going through?' but 'Why did they not act with compassion upon feeling this empathy?'

The Empathy Dolls Approach focuses not only on helping children to identify and explore their own feelings and those of others but to help them grow into confident individuals who are able to act compassionately when witnessing the distress of others. So when considering developing empathy with young children in early years settings what is usually meant is the nurture of all of these skills in response to empathy rather than the development of just empathy itself. It is the development of these skills that forms the foundations and goals of the Empathy Dolls Approach – the ability to attain all round emotional awareness.

Children bond really quickly with the dolls.

1 What is emotional awareness? Why is it important to young children's development?

Children's emotional development occurs alongside and as part of other aspects of their learning and development and yet for many years it has not been given the same priority within early years and school settings as other areas of the curriculum. Recent research and a shift in perceived 'best practice' has resulted in what seems to be a long overdue refocusing on the importance of children's emotional development. As a result, many different terms have been used to describe the physical processes associated with expressing emotions and also the development of positive coping mechanisms to help children to understand and manage their ever changing emotional states. To understand why I have chosen to use the term 'emotional awareness' when considering this approach, it is important that we first identify some of the most commonly used terminology in this field and explore briefly some of the thinking behind the theories.

Most famous of all exponents of positive emotional development is Daniel Goleman, who in his book *Emotional Intelligence – Why it can Matter More than IQ (1996)* identified 'emotional intelligence' as a measure of an individual's ability to both recognise and manage their emotions and also to impact on motivation and relationships with others. It is a term which is now championed by both the education and business worlds worldwide and which identifies five areas for development in building emotional intelligence.

1. Recognising your own emotions
2. Managing your own emotions
3. Self-motivation
4. Recognising emotions in other people and building empathy
5. Building and managing relationships with others

For many years the traditional view was that those individuals who were measured as having a high IQ had the better chance of realising their potential and achieving success in life. The thinking appeared to be that those with high IQ were more likely to go onto higher and further education and therefore to progress further in their chosen career. Goleman argues that the ability to recognise and manage your own emotions as well as recognising and responding appropriately to the emotions of those around you, is more likely to help you reach your full potential in both career and health. It's quite logical when you think about it – if you are able to recognise when you are starting to get angry or stressed and can regulate your emotions accordingly, you are less likely to get into conflict with others and less likely to feel negative about a situation. You will avoid the 'Oh God, not another day at work feeling!' if you are able to identify the triggers of stress or malaise and work positively towards improving the situation. You are more likely to be able to work as a successful and popular team player if you are able to tune in to the feelings of those around you. In interview situations you stand in good stead if you are able to read the emotions of the interviewer and respond appropriately.

Goleman recognises that childhood is a 'window of opportunity' in the development of emotional intelligence and gives great emphasis to the importance of developing emotional skills at a very young age. He is also keen to point out that you are never too old to improve your own individual emotional intelligence, something I am a great believer in and which forms a key part of the foundations to the Empathy Dolls Approach. In order for adults to support children's emotional development they themselves must be open to raising their own self-awareness and to building their emotional interaction and management skills.

The only issue I have with the term emotional intelligence is the use of the word 'intelligence'. The nature of this theory as a means of measurement sets it up as a way of comparing one individual against another and subsequently to one person being perceived as in some way better than another. This approach is probably more palatable to adults, particularly within the business world where emotional intelligence training now supports a multimillion pound business in itself. However, in early years education where the key should, in my opinion, be to help each child to build a positive sense of self and to become a confident and strong individual there seems little room for direct comparison and measurement.

I know I am not the only practitioner to feel this way and I am confident that this mindset led in some part to the development of the term 'emotional literacy' within UK educational establishments. It is a term which is now used widely and not always in the most appropriate context. Sometimes it seems to have been used as a more politically correct or acceptable term for the concept of emotional intelligence when in actual fact the use of the word 'literate' has a particular significance and relates to the development of very specific skills. Its similarities to the traditional view of literacy when linked to the attainment of language and communication skills are profound. To be emotionally literate is to be able to develop the language and communication skills of emotion.

So, as you have probably gathered, I am more comfortable with the use of the term emotional literacy when applied to early years settings. However I still feel that this theory of developing your ability to identify and communicate your emotions does not fully recognise the importance of emotional development in all aspects of early learning. It does not recognise emotional development as a small part of a much bigger whole. Various theorists have, over the years, proposed that early learning should acknowledge much wider educational and spiritual areas. Maslow's theory of a hierarchy of needs (see diagram below) highlights the importance for a child to have their needs met on a number of different levels and this more holistic approach to learning is now widely accepted. As I feel that emotions, their recognition, management and development should be part of a much wider learning picture, I prefer to use the term '**emotional awareness**' as it embraces a concept which can span all aspects of children's development including physical, social, and spiritual. For the purposes of this book I shall use this term to explore the way that we should develop not only our approach to helping children manage their emotions but the way we build supportive learning environments – highlighting the need for continuing professional development.

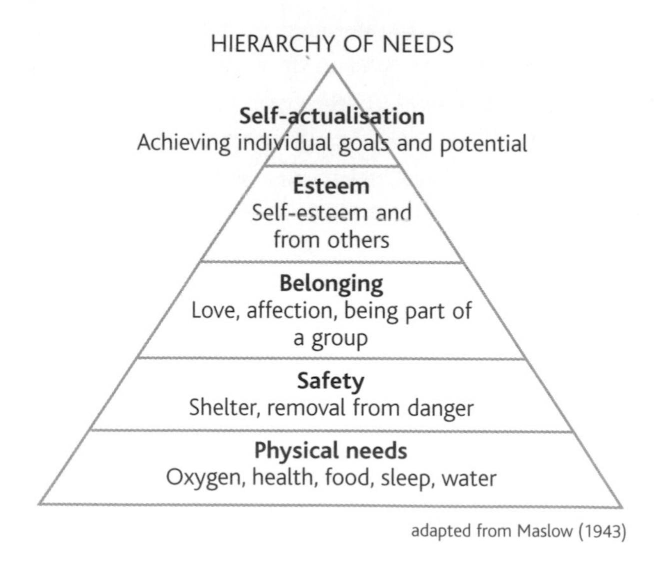

adapted from Maslow (1943)

2 Emotional development and learning in our settings

To understand the importance of creating an 'emotionally aware' environment within your early years setting we first have to understand some of the biological aspects of emotional development. Any descriptions given here are simplified for the purposes of this discussion.

Modern advances in medical technology have allowed us not only to understand which areas of the brain are concerned with the processing of specific emotions, but also, with the aid of sophisticated new brain imaging equipment, we can now actually see the emotional reactions taking place. Our understanding of the relationship between our emotions and our bodies continues to grow year on year.

Science has identified parts of the brain that deal with emotions, the so-called 'emotional brain' and parts that are concerned with learning – 'the learning brain'. It has shown us that the emotional brain has the ability to override the learning brain especially in response to emotions such as fear, anger and stress. To understand this overriding process, what Daniel Goleman in his book *Emotional Intelligence* refers to as an 'emotional hijacking', we have to look a little at the evolution of humans as a species.

Some of us may have glazed over during secondary school science lessons as the teacher droned on about the famous 'fight or flight reaction'. My work with adults working in early years has shown me that many people know the phrase but don't fully understand what happens when the phenomenon kicks in, and subsequently are oblivious to its potential impact on children's learning and development within our settings.

In years gone by when primitive humans spent their days feeding, eating and surviving, the overall objective was the survival of our species. It required these early humans to provide for and protect their young so if you or your family were under threat you had to do something to make sure you all survived to see another day. When facing a threatening situation we instantly feel fear or stress and the emotional part of our brain kicks in and takes priority over thinking or learning elements. It tells our body to prioritise an increase in heart rate to enable blood to be pumped to our extremities including hands and legs. We are then equipped to either 'fight' the potential threat to protect ourselves and our families or to run like the clappers in order to avoid the threat, the so-called 'flight' reaction.

As humans evolved we have, to some extent, retained this emotionally reactive ability and we have probably all experienced it at some time or other. When put in a situation where we are experiencing fear, stress or anger how many of us have felt like we have lost the ability to think rationally? When a car pulls out in front of you on the morning school run, have you felt your heart rate instantly increase, your palms get clammy or your legs get agitated? When an enormous hairy spider scuttles towards you across the bathroom floor does your pulse increase and the need to run from the scene become all encompassing? You are experiencing the emotional brain taking over and preparing you for 'fighting or fleeing'. I know that the spider is not likely to be a threat to the ongoing existence of the human race, although the seriousness of fears and phobias should in no way be underplayed and all emotions are valid and should be acknowledged, but the reaction of our emotional brain is the same as if it were a man-eating arachnid about to steal and eat our offspring! The impact of this potential for emotional hijacking has a huge impact on our provision for developing emotional awareness within our settings.

It is interesting that science has also shown us that we have evolved with some other emotional reactions which are altogether more positive. Again we have to look back in history to see what priorities our ancestors had in their bid for survival to recognise the importance of food and reproduction. In order to ensure future survival of our species there was an obvious need to reproduce and in order to be able to maintain and look after a family you needed to eat to ensure you stayed healthy and strong. These priorities go some way to explaining why the brain reacts with positive emotions during food and sex which then trigger the chemical release of 'feel good' hormones. The result being you generally feel good when you've eaten or had sex and you want to do it again. I don't think I need to elaborate on how we have retained these same emotional reactions as we have evolved, other than it goes some way to explaining the appeal of chocolate!

So chocolate aside, how does this ability to be emotionally hijacked impact upon our practice? Its impact stretches far beyond just giving children opportunities to express or recognise their emotions. Understanding that the parts of the brain concerned with learning and thinking are unable to function properly unless the 'emotional brain' is calm and passive has a huge impact on the physical development of our learning environments. If a child cannot access the thinking and learning parts of their brain because they feel fearful, angry or stressed then the need for providing a calm, safe and supportive environment where children are given space to reflect on their own thoughts and feelings becomes vital. If a child is stressed or afraid it won't matter how exciting or stimulating the learning experiences that you provide are, they won't be able to biologically develop these thought processes.

As well as providing plenty of opportunities to identify emotions and build up children's coping strategies for dealing with their feelings, we also need to be creating spaces within our settings where children are able to relax, be calm and reflect. The development of such quiet reflective spaces can prove challenging within a busy nursery or school but not impossible. I have seen play tents used in a corner, filled with comfortable cushions and pretty fairy lights with soothing music playing quietly in the background. A book corner can serve a dual purpose as a 'chill-out' space with voile drapes hung up to create a sense of cosiness and an aromatherapy diffuser to help provide a multi-sensory relaxation experience. I've even built an underwater cave with a papier-mache frame for the front and some spare dark sheets complete with soothing whale music, shells, soft toy whales and dolphins, and gentle lights projected on the ceiling. However you do it, try to make sure you create a supportive environment where children can feel safe, secure and stress free.

The 'feel good' chemical effect I described earlier just lends weight to what we as early years practitioners know instinctively, that children who

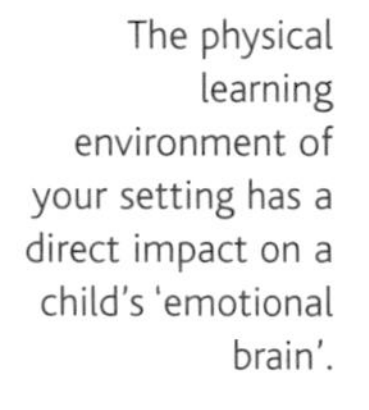

The physical learning environment of your setting has a direct impact on a child's 'emotional brain'.

experience positive feelings will try to recreate the situation that evoked such emotions. By giving praise and encouragement for their triumphs and achievements, no matter how small, children's experiences of positive emotions will drive them to want to repeat activities again and again.

The overriding of emotions associated particularly with anger, stress and fear also has an impact on how we interact with young children when they are in a highly emotional state. The inability to think logically while so emotionally charged means that as practitioners there is no point in trying to reason with a child who is still angry or showing obvious signs of stress or fear. Instead we should offer support and space to enable them to regain a calmer state of mind so that they can access their thinking and learning abilities and then explore more rationally the events which may have led up to them experiencing these emotions. Something worth remembering the next time you try and get a child to see reason when they are really angry or scared.

3 What is an Empathy Doll?

This is a question I am often asked. Many people seem unsure as to whether they need a specific make or type of doll to use with the Empathy Dolls Approach. The easy answer is that this approach is non-doll specific, an Empathy Doll can be **any** doll which the children can identify with as an integral member of their setting. However, experience has shown that dolls with certain characteristics have been more successful than others. Soft-bodied dolls lend themselves to being held and encourage a natural bonding process with children and therefore work much better than hard bodied dolls that are often plastic and cold to the touch. Larger dolls (over 40cm height) tend to work better than smaller dolls as children find they are more likely to accept them as an 'extra member' of the setting than a tiny 'role-play' doll. The temptation is sometimes to think that just because you are working with smaller children you should use a smaller doll. However, it is worth remembering that the principles behind the approach require the doll to stay with a particular group of children throughout their journey through the setting. In other words a doll which originally starts

Soft-bodied dolls lend themselves to being held and cuddled – encouraging a natural bonding process with children.

out with the smaller children in the baby room will remain with those same children as they move up through the setting and will be with them when they are four and five (or even when they are 11 in the case of some primary school settings).

Many of the pictures used in this book show a particular type of doll which was developed in Sweden specifically to encourage the bonding, comforting process with children. In my training sessions we give people dolls so they can get started straight away, hence the reason why these dolls feature heavily in this book. I do however emphasise that I have heard of all sorts of shapes, makes and sizes of dolls being used effectively.

Empathy Dolls have many similarities and differences to Persona Dolls and this seems an opportune stage to give a basic comparative overview of both approaches.

The most common of experiences can evoke the most powerful of feelings.

4 Empathy Dolls and Persona Dolls – similarities and differences

Persona Dolls – a brief history

Using Persona Dolls, as a way of working with early years children, is generally attributed to Kay Taus and her colleagues in the USA in the early 1980s. Kay and her fellow staff members developed a way of working with dolls that addressed issues, which were of particular relevance to the children in their care. With such a wide ranging group of children from many ethnic, cultural and religious backgrounds the challenge was to develop a way to help them look at issues of bullying, racism and discrimination using a story based, problem solving approach. Persona Dolls as an approach is now successfully used throughout the world, highlighting best practice in developing anti-bias approaches in schools and nurseries. In the UK the approach has been championed and developed by Babette Brown through her books and her training company (Persona Dolls Training). Babette has helped to make Persona Dolls the accepted best practice for discussing and developing anti-discriminatory approaches in UK schools and nurseries.

Similarities

At first glance the similarities between the two methods are uncanny and I have had people in the past comment that 'We don't need Empathy Dolls – we already use Persona Dolls'. My usual reply is, 'I'm glad you use Persona Dolls but Empathy Dolls are very different in what they are trying to help you achieve'. I strongly believe there is a place for both approaches in our schools and nurseries as long as we acknowledge that the reasons we are using them are very different. In fact there is nothing stopping an Empathy Doll being further developed to embrace the Persona Dolls approach or a Persona Doll being used as an Empathy Doll with younger children, especially in this world where budgets and expenditure are always under the spotlight!

Both approaches use a doll as their focus and give it a history and a package of information, which remains unique to it as an individual, just like every child and adult we work with. For the Persona Dolls, this package of information is referred to as its 'persona', for Empathy Dolls it is known as the dolls 'story'. The term story seemed appropriate as it relates to the developing information you have about the doll over a long period of time. It highlights that when children first come to our settings we only know a limited amount about each of them. People have even commented that sometimes the only information they have when a child enters the setting is the child's name and the signature of the person who signed all the forms! The Empathy Dolls Approach is developed so that it can start with only the smallest and most limited amount of information and, like a story, as the doll joins in with everything in your setting the knowledge you gain will grow and grow into something interesting, unique and exciting.

Differences

The **first difference** is in the focus of the two approaches. The Empathy Dolls Approach does not take the headline grabbing issues of bullying, racism and discrimination as its focus. It concentrates on the everyday experiences of **all** children and the feelings and emotions which can be evoked by seemingly mundane events. It acknowledges that it is sometimes the most common of experiences that can evoke the most powerful of feelings in young children in our care. In early years settings these feelings are often experienced by children whose understanding far outstrips their ability to communicate how they feel. Added frustrations can then enter the equation and if a child is not given the chance to explore these feelings they can reach a point where the only outlet is through aggressive or anti-social behaviour resulting in damaged self-esteem. It is these frustrations which can be at the route of much of what has commonly become known as the 'terrible two's'. The focus for the Empathy Dolls Approach is very much about '**every child – every day**'.

The **second difference** is the way in which the two approaches introduce the dolls to the children and develop their relationship with them. The Persona Dolls approach is very much story based and relies on a doll visiting the setting to tell the children about something that has happened to them. By its very nature this approach requires the children to instantly take on board the feelings of another i.e. to be able to empathise, which we have already discussed (see page 7) and this may not be easy for younger children to recognise or explore. Also the Persona Dolls approach asks that children discuss the situation raised by the doll and then subsequently explore the anti-bias issues surrounding the experience. This requires the children to be at a stage where they have a certain level of verbal communication skills to enable the discussions and therefore excludes very young children.

Empathy Dolls as an approach was originally developed specifically for early years settings to acknowledge every child's feelings regardless of their ability to communicate. Just because children cannot communicate verbally doesn't mean they can't feel! Imagine the feelings and emotions experienced by a non-talker who is feeling unwell, just learning to crawl and unable to reach a toy or reluctant to lie still for a nappy change (see case study below). This approach acknowledges these feelings and asks that the practitioner be the communicator on behalf of the child, talking through situations and attempting to verbalise their feelings while

Case study

Jake was 10 months old and had just about mastered the art of walking. Not surprisingly this new found skill was something he wanted to make the most of at every possible opportunity. The chance to explore a whole new world that had until now been out of reach! So when Jake's keyworker tried to get him to lay down for a nappy change she encountered an unexpected level of resistance and the changing process began to evoke in Jake a wide range of feelings and emotions. He displayed distress, frustration, anger and to some extent fear at the actions and events surrounding the experience.

A few days later Jake's keyworker decided to try and use Gemma, their Empathy Doll in a bid to make nappy changing a more pleasurable and less stressful experience for Jake. The next time Jake was due for a nappy change she explained to him that Gemma was going to have her nappy changed and asked him if he would help. Jake eagerly agreed, desperate to please. As she proceeded to change the doll's nappy she talked Jake though every aspect of what she was doing and why. 'Gemma is going to lay down here so I can take the nappy off without her falling over. We want to get this horrid wet nappy off her don't we?' etc. She also engaged Jake at every opportunity; letting him pass new nappies, cream and wipes and reassuring him about Gemma's positive feelings about the whole process. Next she turned to Jake and said 'It's your turn now Jake. Is Gemma going to help me like you did?'. As she changed Jake's nappy she continued with the verbalisation and explanation so that he knew exactly what she was doing and why she was doing it. Jake began to relax and the change passed without incident. Jake left holding Gemma's hand happy to have helped and both child and keyworker felt stress free.'

By verbalising the Empathy Doll's feelings in a familiar situation the keyworker had helped the child to work through their emotions as well as making the keyworker more aware of how an everyday task such as nappy changing can affect a child's feelings and emotions.

offering comfort, support and encouragement. This aspect has led to the approach proving successful in supporting many children aged 0-99! I know of projects where the dolls have been developed for use with older adults as part of their dementia care.

The Persona Dolls approach asks that the doll visits the setting, tells its story (often during circle time activities) and then leaves to return again at a later date for further discussions. This is where the **third** and probably most significant difference between the two approaches comes into play. Empathy Dolls do not just visit and then leave – they **stay**! Empathy Dolls join in with everything the children do from snack time and visits to the park, to cutting and sticking and outdoor play. This major difference in approaches is not just for fun but because we have found that by being a part of the children's ongoing everyday lives they are able to build a genuine bond with the dolls, quickly accepting them as another member of the group and subsequently a natural empathic bond forms over time. The eventual outcome is an ability to discuss everyday situations which have affected both the children and the doll. Even very young children find they are able to relate to the perceived feelings of the doll while exploring emotions relating to their own experiences.

Empathy Dolls join in with EVERYTHING in the setting.

It is this 'joining in' element of the Empathy Dolls Approach which is also the single biggest reason I have observed for its possible failure as a

practice in some settings. The idea that a doll becomes a part of all activities within the setting draws on children's inbuilt ability to play imaginatively. It is when the adults involved struggle with the idea of treating the doll like another child that the approach has unravelled. In a society that actively promotes play-based learning for all children but particularly for those in early years, it is key that practitioners are able to access their own imaginative play skills. Not only must they know how children play to learn but they themselves must learn to play. The two examples below illustrate the difference between a nursery setting that has been able to embrace the imaginative play element of the Empathy Dolls Approach and one where the practitioners struggle to step into the child's world of play and creativity.

Case one

In a busy and bustling nursery room a group of young children about two years old are playing happily with a range of floor and role-play activities. In their midst a dark-haired Empathy Doll sits next to two children in the café role-play corner, and the children share their play sandwiches happily with her. After some time a third child decides to join them and struggling to find a third seat pushes the doll onto the floor and sits on her seat. A nursery worker, observing the situation steps in, picks up the doll and hugs her. 'Poor Suky! That would have hurt her, pushing her off the chair like that. I think she's a bit sad now'. The practitioner not only pointed out the doll's feelings but reacted quickly to the doll's situation, similarly to if it had been a child.

Case two

Visiting one nursery a few years ago I was pleased to observe some fabulous work with the Empathy Dolls in a number of different rooms. Displays included pictures of the dolls and pegs carrying dolls' clothes were interspersed with the children's coat pegs. The dolls had been truly integrated and accepted as an important part of this setting. However, on moving into the toddler room I was puzzled to see their Empathy Doll perched on top of a high cupboard, obviously there so as to be out of reach of the children. As I looked around the room I noticed that there was little sign of the integration of the dolls that I had observed elsewhere in the nursery. The walls, although covered with pictures of the children involved in activities, displayed no images of the dolls and depicted no interactions between dolls and children. I quizzed one of the nursery workers as to why the doll was on top of the cupboard. 'Oh!' she replied, 'It's because in here the children just throw her around by her hair so we don't use her anymore!'

5 Common misunderstandings when using Empathy Dolls

Having explained in some depth what an Empathy Doll 'is' it may seem pointless to consider the negative side of the argument. However, it's important to remember that you are working with children's individual feelings and often fragile emotions. We should never forget what a privileged position this is and how much influence we have on the lives of the children we interact with each and every day. If the approach is not implemented in a structured, well thought out and considered fashion the potential to do damage to these feelings and emotions is only too obvious. This section is not supposed to frighten, shock or put you off using the approach – it is just aimed at making you think carefully before implementing your plans.

There are three golden rules of what **not** to do when developing your Empathy Doll. They are as follows:

1. Dolls should **not** be used to react to negative situations.
2. Dolls should **not** be used as a tool for encouraging confrontation.
3. Dolls should **not** be a direct reflection of any one child in your care.

Having been bought up to believe that mistakes are there to be used as tools for future learning, I think that the most powerful way of conveying 'how not to do it' is to relay some of my own observations in relation to these rules.

Make sure you plan when and how to use the dolls

Case study

A teacher sits in front of her class with a doll sat on her lap. She gently holds the doll as she starts to tell the children what has happened to the doll and how he is feeling as a result.

'Jack is feeling a bit sad this afternoon. He was playing outside and some of the other children wouldn't let him join in with their game. In fact, some of them were calling him some quite nasty names.'

Adults talk on behalf of the doll not for the doll.

So what is wrong with this situation? On the face of it – nothing! The teacher has used the doll in the correct manner, talking on behalf of the doll and not pretending to be the doll. With Empathy Dolls there is no need to hone your ventriloquist skills to find a voice for the doll! This will also avoid confusion if different practitioners, especially male and female carers, are using the doll as its voice will change with them and this will not worry the children.

So, if the teacher in question is using the correct vocal approach, what is it that is wrong with her discussion? Was it the fact that she had used the doll to address a negative situation? No. The dolls are great for helping children to identify and work through some of the negative or less comfortable feelings they may be experiencing. However, always remember that no child goes through life only experiencing negative feelings and emotions. Children need to be given opportunities to explore a balance of negative and positive situations. This may seem obvious but putting it into practice takes planning and its all too easy to slip into the trap of negativity. One teacher told me how she hadn't even realised she was doing it until one of the children asked her about their Empathy Doll, 'Why does everything bad always happen to Rosie?'

Another professional once claimed not to be an advocate of the Empathy Dolls Approach as she 'didn't believe in having a naughty child as a focus!'. After much discussion and delving it turned out that every time her doll had been presented to the children it had done something wrong!

A prime example of the importance of fully understanding the role of Empathy Dolls before embarking upon their use and of **planning** when and how to use them

In this particular situation, the mistake was in the teacher's **timing.** The incident she was referring to had actually happened less than an hour beforehand. She had used the Empathy Doll as a tool to react to a negative situation. We all know that the children we work with are not stupid and in this case they knew exactly who had been involved in the original incident and so their focus was distracted away from the doll. The children knew who had been the perpetrators and they knew who had been the victim. The teacher might as well have not even had the doll as the children's focus was clearly not on it but on those they knew had been involved in the incident. This is in complete contrast to the Empathy Dolls Approach which believes that every child has the right to explore their feelings and emotions in any given situation, without fear of ridicule or reprisal. In this case the children who had perpetrated the incident had just as much right to be given a chance to identify and find ways of working through their feelings and emotions as the child who had become the victim.

That isn't to say that you cannot use the dolls as a stimulus for discussion about negative situations, but just make sure that you **plan** the discussions so that they are long enough after the event in question so that no child is left feeling – 'they're all talking about me'. There is a fine line between what you want to achieve which is children thinking 'I've felt like that before… it must be ok to feel like that' and a child feeling as if the eyes of the world are upon them.

Be careful of the language you use when discussing the dolls

I am a great believer that labels stick and that children are too young to be labelled. Human nature means that we tend to adapt our behaviour to labels, even if we don't intend to.

I once knew a little girl who lost her father suddenly when she was just four years old. Her widowed mother was left with the young girl and her two week old baby brother to bring up on her own. The little girl's mum was disabled and spent much of her time confined to a wheelchair and despite holding down a part-time job the whole family relied on benefits to survive. Both children were eligible for free school meals and the little girl suffered from a wide range of allergies, asthma and eczema.

This child was given so many labels and some people may have reacted differently to her because of one or more of them – 'single parent family', 'disabled parent', 'low income', 'free school meals', and 'asthmatic' to name but a few.

Or was she just a little girl from a loving supportive, close-knit family who loved painting and drawing, always had her head in a book, loved playing football and dreamed of being a teacher? She was the latter – I know this because that little girl was me!

And yet I have witnessed practitioners label dolls (and possibly children) as naughty, aggressive, from single parent families, etc. I believe children should not be judged by labels. As professionals we need to take the time to look at what actually might be causing the child to behave in a certain way or how a label might have a negative impact on a child's self-esteem.

One child psychologist told me that she was frequently called to assess children with behaviour difficulties and when she asked 'Have you spent a day with the child to see what your nursery or routine looks like from their point of view?' received the surprised reply 'No!' She was fed up with dealing with people who hadn't even considered the possibility that something they were doing might be perpetuating the behaviour or that the physical environment might not be helping the individual child.

Children are children and they react to feelings and emotions evoked by things which are going on in their lives. It is up to us to try and help them cope with whatever life is throwing at them and to enable them to respond to the world in the best way they can to allow them to grow to their full potential. As Maggie Dent says 'Nurturing kids' hearts and souls is the most effective way of helping build a healthy self-esteem and self concept, and this begins early in life.' (M. Dent 2005).

Food for thought

The Power of words

A group of frogs were travelling through the woods and two of them fell into a deep pit. All of the other frogs gathered around the pit. When they saw how deep the pit was, they told the two frogs that they were as good as dead.

The two frogs ignored the comments and tried to jump up out of the pit with all their might. The other frogs kept telling them to stop, that they were as good as dead. Finally one frog took heed, and gave up. He fell down and died.

The other frog continued to jump as hard as he could. Once again the crowd of frogs yelled at him to stop the pain and just give up and die. He jumped even harder and finally he jumped up out of the pit.

When he got to the other frogs they said 'Didn't you hear us?'. The frog explained to them that he was deaf. He thought the other frogs had been encouraging him all the time he was in the pit!

This story teaches two lessons:

1. There is power of life and death in the tongue. An encouraging word to someone who is down can lift them up and help them to make it through the day.
2. A destructive word to someone who is down can be what it takes to kill them.

It is sometimes hard to understand that an encouraging word can go such a long way. Anyone can speak words that have the potential to rob another of the spirit to continue in difficult times. Be careful of what you say.

'Speak life to those who cross your path.' *Dent 2005*

Don't be tempted to make your doll a direct reflection of any one individual child

It is easy to see how sometimes elements of this approach might benefit one particular child in your care, or may have proven useful when working with a child in the past. With this in mind it is understandable that some practitioners fall into the trap of making their doll too closely resemble an individual child.

We know that it is important that no individual child feels under the spotlight or picked upon. We all, I am sure, can remember at least one incident in our past where someone has asked a question or demanded that you do something leaving you feeling as though the eyes of the world were upon you? Thrust into those situations many of us erect barriers and feel reluctant to participate. Children are the same and if made to feel like they are the focus of attention, they are likely to put up defences leading to the opposite result to that you are trying to achieve. You want children to feel comfortable to explore, explain and express their personal experiences and feelings.

The example given on page 29 only goes to highlight how, with the best of intentions, it is easy to develop your doll with too personal a focus.

This example could not be further from the roots of what the Empathy Dolls Approach aims to achieve. As adults working with young children, it is all too easy to try and change the world overnight but this approach is not the tool for doing so. So be careful not to make your doll reflect too closely any of the children in your setting. When developing your doll's

Case study

A nursery class were expecting a new child to join them in the very near future. The little boy in question was coming to the setting from an asylum seeker background and the staff felt sure that an Empathy Doll could benefit him and the other children during the settling in process. After much discussion the staff had, quite rightly, identified certain common issues which the children could explore with the new child. These included 'starting a new school', 'moving house' and 'making new friends' – situations experienced by many of the children in their care, so allowing more than one child to potentially benefit from the Empathy Dolls approach.

With this excellent attitude in place the staff team set to work building the initial identity and background story for the doll but this is where it all started to go wrong! Instead of creating a unique individual with potential to help and support lots of children with elements of many children woven into its story, the staff chose a doll with a similar skin tone to the new child and developed a story which mirrored exactly his background. They then began working with the children to explore the common issues they had already identified over a period of two to three weeks until the day came when the little boy was due to join them.

On that day, not only was this vulnerable child starting nursery, but he was in a strange country with only a few family members around him and none of his friends. He was walking into a strange building with different routines. He was encountering new adults and children and being asked to enter a setting with which he was completely unfamiliar and one in which the majority of people were speaking a language which was not his first language.

Personally, I think this situation is more than enough for anyone to have to cope with emotionally, let alone a small child. Yet on that morning not only did he have to deal with all of this but upon entering the nursery the better part of 22 children, over the morning, commented along the lines of 'Ooh you're just like James!' (referring to their Empathy Doll). So he was expected to cope with a barrage of emotions evoked by his first day at a new nursery and he then had to deal with the feeling that he was the centre of everyone's attention!

story choose elements of every child you have ever known, every child you will ever know and every child you will never know. Put them all together and develop your own unique individual who can support many different children in your setting and who will help them to know it is '**okay to be me**'!

6 Developing your Empathy Doll's story

'Seeing the world from the child's perspective is an essential first step to learning...' *(Gordon, M. 2005)*

The key to this approach is the belief and understanding that children don't always see the world the way we do. Maybe we can learn something from them in developing our own approaches to building positive learning environments? When beginning to develop your doll's story you must first remember why you are using this approach. You are embarking on a way of working which aims to help children develop their emotional awareness and enrich their positive sense of self. To be able to work towards these goals it is vital that you, the practitioner, take the time to see the world through the eyes of the children you are working with. This is something which many practitioners I meet are confident that they already do, but when questioned further and asked to look more closely I find many are actually seeing the world as they think children 'should' see it or even just assuming that children see things in the same way as they do.

Looking at life through a child's eyes

One practitioner's response, when asked how often she took the time to sit in her setting and look at how exciting it all appeared from the child's height and perspective, summed up the need for this focus. She replied sadly, 'We look everyday... but we don't see'.

Common, everyday experiences look completely different when viewed through a child's eyes. I think the following story on page 31 highlights the misconception of children's views of the world brilliantly.

There are many, many things which make us all different, unique and wonderful in our own right. The Empathy Dolls approach focuses on getting children to accept that no matter what the combination of these things is it's **'okay to be me'**. It takes the stand that children are more than just the colour of their skin, their family background, religion or physical abilities. It focuses on celebrating all aspects of an individual as part of what goes to make us all special.

In considering this uniqueness when developing your doll's story you may wish to think about many aspects of their individual character including those areas explored below, in each case remembering to view

Case study

A young woman having lost her father suddenly some years beforehand, decided to take her young daughter to visit her grandad's grave having never had the chance to meet him before he died. They had talked a lot about 'Grandad' and the fact that they were going to a special place to visit him. Upon arrival at the cemetery with its array of graves and memorials the mother braced herself for the onslaught of sadness and other negative emotions she was expecting her daughter to experience. Then turning to her mother with a gloomy look on her face the little girl remarked, 'Mummy I knew I should have bought my bucket and spade!' She had viewed the cemetery not as a sad or morbid place (as her mother had expected) but as a colourful garden ripe for a bit of weeding!

the world through the eyes of the children. It's important to try and avoid the all too easy trap of projecting as many negative aspects and experiences as you can imagine onto the one doll. Our inbuilt instinct to focus on the negative or the 'politically correct' can mean that before you know it you have a doll who is blind in one eye, has a limp, lives with a single heroin addict mother, with a father in prison and a grandad who's just run off with the milkman! Seriously, the approach needs to acknowledge that although children do come into contact with negative experiences, they also enjoy the positive things in life and all the enriching experiences they bring.

The easy thing to do when given a tool such as an Empathy Doll is to try and solve all of the world's problems single-handed, instead of actually looking at the small issues that affect our children as they go about their lives everyday.

Family background

Remember your doll does not have to have a single parent just because you feel you need to represent a cross-section of society through the dolls in your setting. However, if you find that a significant proportion of the children you are working with do come from a single parent background then this is likely to evoke feelings which your children can relate to and your doll would be justified in having a single parent. When considering your doll's family background you have to look at the way in which everyday aspects of family life can affect children emotionally.

- **Parents** Does your doll have one, two, three or even four parents (if their birth parents have split and found new partners)? It is easy to give your doll a single parent or newly separated parents and to focus on all of the negative issues you perceive in these situations. When considering this from a child's perspective you begin to realise that not all children experience negative feelings and emotions in these circumstances. A child with a single parent may have a really close bond with their mum or dad and spend more quality time with them than if they were in a two parent family where both parents work long hours. A child who spends time with both separated parents on a regular basis may get to see their parents in a more calm, relaxed atmosphere than a home full of arguments.

- **Siblings** Does your doll have older or younger siblings (both of which can have an emotional impact on children's feelings and their subsequent behaviour)? Children with older siblings may be used to being treated as the baby of the family, with brothers and sisters ready and willing to always step in and talk on their behalf, effectively 'mothering' them. A child used to this kind of situation, when placed in an early years environment, may be perceived as 'shy' or 'quiet'. When you look past the labels at the child's view of the world where you aren't used to being able to talk for yourself – it takes on a whole new perspective! They could be the most confident child in the world, just not used to being able to express themselves without someone else jumping in!

The case below is a classic example of how we are all too quick to jump to conclusions instead of looking at the bigger picture from the child's perspective.

Case study

One lady told me how she had been the youngest of a very large, happy, close-knit family. Her mother had been quite dismayed to be questioned one day about her parenting skills and whether she had in some way been neglecting the youngest child? Apart from her obvious anger at what she perceived as an attack on her abilities as a mother, the lady was keen to find out what had sparked this particular line of enquiry. It all stemmed from a number of incidents observed in nursery. During snack and meal times the youngest daughter had appeared to be overly eager to eat whatever was placed in front of her, often grabbing food before being asked. The practitioners had concluded that she must be so hungry because she wasn't receiving proper meals at home!

The reality couldn't have been further from the truth. In the lady's own words 'As part of a very large family you soon learn to engage in survival tactics. Meals and playtimes can become a bit of a bun fight and you end up grabbing whatever you can get your hands on – before someone grabs your toy or portion of food!'

Looking at the incident from the child's perspective – the child wasn't starving or even hungry at nursery – she was just deploying the survival tactics she had learnt from being the youngest of a large, caring and boisterous family! Oh how wrong we can sometimes be!

A note of caution! Don't shy away from being aware of the signs of potential neglect and abuse in very young children. I have sadly worked with enough children in the past who have been genuine victims and the effects on those children haunt me to this day. Better to be safe than sorry.

- **Grandparents and extended family** Does your doll have contact with grandparents or other family members on a regular basis? With ever changing demands on parent's time and work commitments, and the government pushing for parents to return to the workplace, children find themselves in the care of others. If parents work long hours it is often the grandparents who step in and bring the child to the setting or attend assemblies, etc. We have to acknowledge the impact that relationships with the extended family can have on children emotionally. Do grandparents have different expectations of behaviour from the child? A child who is used to two different sets of ground rules will naturally test the boundaries to see what they can get away with and it is only to be expected that this same child will then do exactly the same when placed in your own setting. Not because they are 'naughty', 'aggressive' or 'antisocial' but because their life situation dictates that that is what they are used to doing.

A child who comes from a single parent family, living on benefits in council accommodation may have issues and emotions they have to recognise and deal with on an everyday basis but equally so has the child who has two affluent, working parents who may not get home until after bedtime and who may try desperately to make amends for lost hours by trying to cram as much as they possibly can into the weekends. Children are like us, they need their own quiet time and reflective space! Look out for the child who crawls through the door of the setting on a Monday morning exhausted from the weekend events and desperately seeking a quiet place to be on their own!

Physical characteristics

When considering the physical characteristics to give your doll you really do have to try to see the world from a child's perspective. Children don't tend to see the colour of someone's skin or whether they are in a wheelchair, they are more interested in someone's newly spiked hairdo or their latest coat or shoes. The following examples highlight the differences in perception beautifully!

Case one

A mainstream nursery setting had recently been teamed with a special needs school setting with the aim to integrate the two and share experiences and friendships. Prior to the first visit the staff of the mainstream setting were discussing their preparations and a question arose about whether they should say anything to their children about the walking aids, wheelchairs, speech aids, hearing-aids, etc. that the visiting children would bring with them. The discussion went on for a while and they finally decided not to mention anything before the visit. The day came and was a fantastic success and activities were thoroughly enjoyed by all. A return visit was already planned before everyone was back on the minibus!

I can't help but be amazed that when reviewing the visit, all of the staff from the mainstream setting were genuinely surprised that not one of their children commented on the array of physical aids used by the children from the special needs school. They couldn't understand that their children didn't notice the wheelchairs or the hearing-aid – they just saw other children to play with!

Case two

A nursery which I have the pleasure of working with on a regular basis, and who have embraced the Empathy Dolls Approach wholeheartedly, recounted an incident which they used during a recent OFSTED inspection as an indicator of their general ethos across the whole setting. Having previously attended one of my workshops the nursery had successfully established a black doll in one of their rooms. Patrick was busy having a myriad of adventures with the children both in the nursery and at their homes on sleepovers! He was a fully integrated member of the setting and his profile was testament to the fantastic experiences being had by all.

More recently another member of staff attended another training event and took away another doll for use in the setting. This time the new addition was a very pale skinned little girl with white hair and almost albino features. Upon introducing Lucy to the children one child's instant reaction was, 'Is Lucy Patrick's sister?' As the nursery manager was quick to reiterate with the OFSTED inspector, she thought this illustrated their ethos beautifully. A setting where everyone was accepted as themselves, where people were much more than just the colour of their skin or their physical ability and where children were just children!

Case three

A little girl, aged 7, had recently started school in a new area in Bradford, West Yorkshire. The child was placed in a class where the majority of children were of Asian origin and she began to make some fantastic new friends.

One day she was chattering away at home telling all who would listen about her recent adventures with her new best friend: a little girl with a classically Asian sounding name. Her uncle who had some less than 'politically correct' views of society, commented to the child, 'I bet with a name like that your mate's got brown skin?'. The child stopped mid-flow, thought hard, looked at her uncle and said confidently, 'No!'.

The child didn't see the colour of her friend's skin – she just saw an individual with whom to experience all the wonders of being seven in today's world. A prime example of adults making skin colour an issue instead of allowing the children to view the world their way.

Likes and dislikes

When devising your Empathy Doll's character take care not to concentrate exclusively on possible likes and forget to come up with some dislikes. To create a more rounded personality you will need to think of dislikes too and see them as an important part of the doll's make-up.

When describing children's likes and dislikes I have observed, over many years, a phenomenon which repeats itself time and time again. After much discussion with individual practitioners and parents I can only conclude that what I have observed is due to two main factors. Firstly, the intonation of the English language and especially the use of the word 'but', and secondly, the effects of years of government initiatives and policies focusing on the latest educational issues. I often hear comments such as these:

'He really likes playing outside on the bikes and trikes but he doesn't like sitting still on the carpet'.
'She really likes drawing and role-play but she doesn't like carrots'.
'He really likes painting but doesn't like sharing'.

In each of these examples the description conveys the implication that somehow it is wrong for children to **not like** things! I always ask the adults I work with the same question and it is something you will have to ask yourself if you too are to embrace this approach: 'Do you as an adult like everything?' The answer will always be a resounding **no**!

As adults we find it easy to accept that part of what makes us who we are as individuals is not only the things which we like but also the things which we don't like. Yet as childcare practitioners we somehow expect children to like everything and to embrace all the wonderful experiences which we spend hours preparing with equal and copious amounts of enthusiasm. Why do we find it so hard to accept that part of what makes children unique individuals is both the things they like and the things they dislike? We need to respect these differences as much as we do the colour of a child's skin, their hair colour or family situation. Ultimately, the world will not stop turning just because a child does not like carrots! It is not the end of the world if a child does not like peas or dislikes playing in the sand! This may sound logical but I still come across settings where practitioners insist on trying to get a child who obviously doesn't like peas to eat them or insisting that a child who doesn't like the feel of the sand to go outside and play in it! Why do we try and make children do things they don't like doing? What emotional upheaval are we guilty of instigating when we fail to acknowledge the all-round uniqueness of the individuals we work alongside each and every day?

Does your setting promote a positive attitude to children's dislikes as well as likes? Do children feel comfortable telling you that they don't like something? Do they feel happy that we are all unique individuals and we all have things that we don't like... including the adults? Why is this element of the approach so key to the emotional development of young children? Consider the following...

An Empathy doll has a unique personality and likes and dislikes – just like each child in your setting.

Exercise

Make a list of all the things you have ever done in your life in order to avoid doing something you don't like. Experience has shown me that your list might include some or all of the following:

- Distraction – doing or saying something unrelated to divert attention away from the thing you don't like doing.
- Throwing a tantrum – for adults this can include shouting, screaming and the obligatory throwing of a saucepan or two!
- Faking illness – getting out of doing things with a mystery stomach ache, or a sudden migraine.
- Sulking – going quiet and not wanting to talk to anyone or refusing to discuss the situation concerned.
- Going to the toilet – again and again!

Now look back at your list and see if you have ever witnessed any of the above in the children you have worked with? Ever thought that there might be a good reason for them throwing themselves on the floor screaming, knocking over a friend's building blocks, a sudden sick feeling or the need to go to the toilet again?

Faced with the situation where a small boy doesn't like going outside to play on the bikes and trikes because its noisy, scary and everyone runs around really fast, would your setting allow the child the opportunity to express his dislike as he is being herded out of the door into the play area? Or would the child feel he had to deploy some alternative behaviour tactics to avoid being made to do something he disliked?

Avoiding portraying dislikes as a negative trait is often easier said than done. Not using the word 'but' before describing a trait can help as most comments following 'but' are by the very nature and intonation of the English language perceived as negative. Dislikes and things we are not as skilled at make up a big part of the unique individual we are. By completing the above exercise you will be able to see how important it is to portray these traits more positively.

Things we are good at and things we are not so good at

As has been discussed in the previous section the combination of language intonation, and a need to follow current trends in education policy, can sometimes cause us to portray certain aspects of a child's character in a negative light. When it comes to talking about the things that children are good at and not so good at it is easy to find yourself saying:

‘He’s really good at playing on the bike and trikes but not so good at sharing.’

‘She’s fabulous at creative painting and drawing but isn’t so good at sitting still on the carpet.’

The first thing I would say to any practitioner uttering words such as these is:

‘Are you good at everything? No? Neither are children!’

Be aware of this when deciding on aspects of your Empathy Doll’s character. What will he/she be good at or not so good at?

For instance, I love to draw and write. On the other hand, I have suffered from asthma since I was a small child and find it difficult to run around in team sports like some of my friends. I try not to beat myself up about my physical inabilities. The things I am good at form just as much a part of the unique individual that I am as do the things I am less adept at and should be valued equally.

It is this change in perception and a conscious move towards portraying all aspects of a child’s character as a positive part of who they are, that underpins the Empathy Dolls Approach. This is important especially in a world which offers a bombardment of media and peer pressure to be like

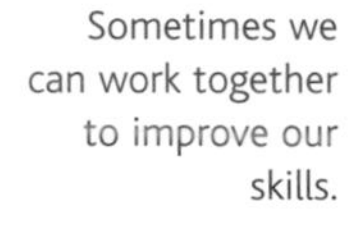

Sometimes we can work together to improve our skills.

everyone else, to look a certain way, and to own certain things; alongside an education system with its constant system of testing that encourages children to compare their abilities against each other rather than celebrate individual success. There is more need than ever to let all of the children we come into contact with know that they are all unique, fabulous individuals. We need to help them understand that part of that uniqueness is that we all have things we are not so good at. Some things we can work together to improve and some things we cannot change but are no less a part of us.

So the previous observations can be rephrased to reflect a much more positive approach to individual uniqueness:

'He's really good at playing outside on the bikes and trikes. He is trying really hard to share his toys and games with other children.'

'She's fabulous at creative painting and when she gets a bit fidgety on the carpet she helps me with some of my special jobs.'

So, whatever character traits you allocate to you doll during the story building process, please remember you are not developing a doll to solve everything. It is okay for your doll to display things that they are good at and not so good at just like a child.

7 Introducing your doll into your setting

'One of the most important gifts we can offer young children is a positive view of themselves.' *M.Dowling 2005*

Now that you have developed your doll's story you can prepare to introduce your new unique doll into your setting. This process is one which needs to be planned and is not without its practical implications.

The nature of the approach asks that the doll becomes an integral member of the setting and participates in any activities which the children are involved in. This can include snack time, outdoor play, toileting and, in the case of childminder settings, attending parent and toddlers groups. The reality of your doll joining in with all tasks within the setting means that a further characteristic worth considering when picking which doll to use is the ability for it to be washed, particularly when taking part in messy play activities.

Case study

A cautionary tale

A large inner city Children's Centre had embraced the Empathy Dolls Approach whole-heartedly. The dolls were established across the setting and in one of their two nurseries there were Empathy Dolls in every keyworker group.

One of the keyworkers was planning to attend the Athens Olympics in 2000. The excitement in the setting was heightened by the knowledge that one of their dolls, Harry, would be going with her to Greece to witness this historic event. For weeks prior to her trip the children had discussed the Olympic games, looked at maps of Greece, built an airport role-play area and helped Harry to pack his suitcase.

A few days before they were due to fly, the keyworker was leading a group discussion when she noticed that her colleague was handling the doll carefully with a look of obvious distaste on her face. Upon closer inspection it was discovered that a large head louse was exploring the doll's head! For obvious reasons, and after the mandatory 'there are head lice in our setting' letter had been sent home, the doll went into the washing machine. This left no time for it to dry before the plane for Athens. Some quick thinking and a similar looking doll from another part of the setting was sent off on his travels around Europe, leaving Harry to be dried and then stored in a cupboard. All was fine until one naturally inquisitive child opened the cupboard and found the unclothed doll. Pandemonium ensued as the children reacted emotionally and very vocally! It was quickly explained to the children that this was in fact the original doll's cousin and that he was just playing hide and seek in the cupboard. As for the lack of clothing issue, I think we have all met at least one child in our careers who would prefer to lose their clothes at every given opportunity!

The moral of this story is do not under estimate the power and strength of the attachment the children can build up for the Empathy Dolls within a very short space of time. At all times treat the dolls as you would the children (or at least make sure the children don't see the dolls in the washing machine, tumble dryer or airing cupboard!)

Before introducing your doll into your setting

Having developed your doll's story as a team to maximise impact and effectiveness, you now need to record the doll's story somewhere prominent and in a way that allows you to add to it as additional information becomes available. In the UK the requirement to keep individual profiles for all children lends itself brilliantly to this element of the doll's development. Create a portfolio for the doll in the same format as your existing ones. Use this to record the doll's story so far, include a photograph of the doll and display it so that all individuals coming into contact with the doll can access the information. The doll's story should be accessible to staff, visitors and parents alike. They all need to know about the doll and be on board for the approach to work successfully.

Make sure that whenever additional information is added it is recorded within the profile and is shared on a regular basis with staff. Try meeting for just five minutes a week to read through any additions and to refresh staff's enthusiasm to keep the momentum of the approach going.

Both before introducing your doll, and regularly afterwards, I would emphasise the importance of working in partnership with the parents. I have found that settings where the approach has been particularly successful have taken the time to let parents know something of the theory behind the approach and to explain how it will benefit their children. An explanation of how the approach will work within the setting helps the parents to feel they are active participants in their child's care and enables them to join in showing interest in the doll's activities.

I recently heard how one setting told the children that the Empathy Doll was staying at home as he had chickenpox, something most of the children had also suffered from in recent weeks. When the doll returned the staff were delighted when one morning a parent known for not being the most enthusiastic participant in nursery activities stopped the keyworker in her child's room to comment, 'I'm really glad to see that Ruben is back from being off with chickenpox'. Small steps achieve big goals!

Starting off

As with the arrival of any new member at your setting, the introduction of the doll needs to be planned and carried out over a period of time to ensure children are comfortable with its presence and happy to play with and alongside the doll. I would suggest a number of short visits over a period of one or two weeks to 'settle the doll in'. At each visit give the children a little bit more detail about the doll and increase the opportunities for it to join in with the children's activities. By the time the doll starts permanently, the children should have begun to build a bond with the doll and be happy with it joining in with them.

For the Empathy Dolls Approach to work the doll has to become a fully integrated member of the setting. To ensure this is the case, make sure that the doll has everything the same as the children. For instance, the doll will

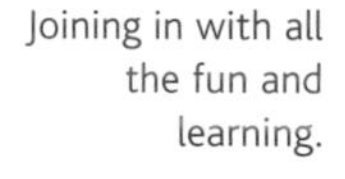
Joining in with all the fun and learning.

need its own coat peg its own basket or drawer to store belongings, and will need to be included in photographs around the setting. If self-registration occurs in your setting make sure provision is made for your doll to be included.

By making the doll a very visible and prominent member of the setting, and only when this is firmly established, you will be able to start planning to send the doll home on 'sleepovers' with the children. You will then begin to see the benefits of the dolls in bridging the home/setting divide and their effective use as a tool for working in partnership with parents (see page 51).

Frequently asked questions

Introducing the Empathy Dolls Approach into your setting is not without its practical implications and many of the same questions come up time and again in my work with early years professionals. However it is worth noting that as the approach is built on the individuality of every child there can be no definitive right or wrong answers to these questions. How the approach actually works within your setting will very much depend upon the individual children in your care and can even differ from one room to another within the same setting. All I can offer is the wisdom of the experience of those who have already tried it. You will know your children and will hopefully find a way of implementing the approach that works for you and them.

How does the doll come into the setting each day?

This is very much dependent upon the type of setting you work in and the story you have developed for your doll, i.e is your doll attending full-time or part-time? I have seen some great ways of ensuring the doll is ready to be integrated into the activities and adventures of the day within the nursery/preschool or school setting:

- One nursery sets up activities and equipment each morning prior to the children's arrival. As part of their preparation they dress the dolls in their outfits for the day (no child comes to nursery in the same clothes everyday!) and then the dolls are strategically placed next to or already taking part in some of the activities. As the children arrive they just fall into working alongside the dolls as they choose their tasks for that session. The dolls being the first to arrive and the last to leave the setting can alleviate many questions about the dolls' overnight activities and their family!

- Another nursery has a doll which lives near to one of the keyworkers and gets a lift in with them every morning. That's fine as long at the key worker remembers to belt the doll into their car seat or booster!

I have heard many creative approaches to this question, and the most complex has to be the one detailed below, which I think reflects the commitment some individuals have to making this approach work for their children.

- In a busy and bustling multi-adult childminder setting, the day begins with one practitioner leaving the setting via a side door, running round to the front of the setting and ringing the doorbell. A second childminder then answers the door where they find the doll and welcome him in as if he had just been dropped off by his parents! At the end of the day the reverse process goes into action and the doll leaves through the front door with all the other children.

I know of childminders who have fostered or adopted a doll or who have accepted the doll as an extended family member coming to stay for an indefinite period of time. This approach appears to negate the need to hide the doll overnight in the airing cupboard and has proven useful in helping a practitioner's own children through stressful or emotional periods.

What happens if they say 'It's only a doll'?

This is a reaction which you will probably come into contact with at some point from one of a number of sources. It may be asked by the children involved with the doll, older children in the school, childminder's own children, or parents and other significant adults.

The Empathy Dolls Approach itself recognises that everyone is an individual and we all have opinions and views which should be acknowledged and valued. If a child working with the doll comes out with this statement, acknowledge their observation and move on with little or no further explanation and you will rarely have an issue on your hands. The approach never claims that the doll is human, and should always be recognised as a doll that happens to come to your setting. However, I have found that many people who ask this question prior to working with Empathy Dolls are often dealing with their own inability to recognise the doll as an integral member of the setting and are subsequently surprised at the children's ability to accept the doll in the same way as their friends and peers.

Older children often comment after they reach what I call the 'Father Christmas age' – when they start to question if Father Christmas is real! If you try to include these children in the development process, as you build the doll's story from scratch, they are then engaged and involved with the doll and the question is less likely to crop up. If it does just use the same approach as for younger children, acknowledge and move on!

One childminder emailed me to say that having been concerned that her ten year old son might spoil the approach in her setting with questions like this, she took time to explain to him that she was using the approach to help the little ones talk about their feelings. This was a simple explanation which he seemed happy to accept. She then spent two weeks exploring and developing the doll's story in partnership with her son. By the end of the two weeks the boy knew pretty much everything there was to know about the doll, including what kind of cars the doll's parents were driving! Being a part of this development process, teamed with an honest explanation of the approach meant that the older child was fully involved and enthusiastic for the doll to be introduced to the younger children.

Parents and other significant adults require a whole other approach to avoid this kind of comment and to give a satisfactory answer. If it comes from this source my instinct would be that there has not been enough preparation before introducing the doll into your setting (see page 42). If it has been asked by an adult outside of the child's immediate circle of care this calls for positive conviction from the practitioner and a firm, simple explanation as to why you are using the Empathy Dolls Approach with the children. However, be aware that this approach is not for everyone and some adults will not understand or accept why you are using this method to try to develop confident, well-rounded young people who are proud to be themselves.

As the approach becomes more common place in your area you will hopefully find people become more accepting. When wheeling my young son around a well-known supermarket sat happily next to our own Empathy Doll, Molly, people were happy to acknowledge both my son and his companion and there were rarely raised eyebrows or comments from adults. This is because the Empathy Dolls approach has been in place in Leeds settings for nearly five years now and is recognised across the entire city. Championed by Judy Dawes, the authority's commitment to the approach is reflected in their purchase of an Empathy Doll for every local authority early years setting in the city.

Does the doll have to join in with everything?

In the beginning the answer is definitely **yes**! This is how the dolls become integral to all that you do in your setting.

However, once established and proving useful, I concede that you may like to change a few things. The approach was never meant to create added stress or pressure for anyone and I appreciate that occasionally the practicalities of trailing your doll along with you at every turn may not be in the best interests of the children or your own sanity! It is okay once in a while when leaving to go on a walk to say, 'Susie isn't feeling very well today so she's going to stay behind with the children in the baby room and have a little snuggle up on the sofa while we go to the park'.

Although, you may find that the children will insist on the doll being involved much more than you expect. One nursery nurse commented to me 'I thought you were kidding when you said the children would ensure the doll was involved. But the other day I sat the children down for snack as always and three of the six children chorused that I had left Rachel behind! Whilst retrieving her from the book corner the other three were busy getting her a chair, cup and plate!'

Do I need any extra equipment?

Easy answer… yes! Does it need to be expensive… no!

You will have to consider if you need an extra highchair, booster seat, coat peg, etc. to ensure the doll is treated as another member of the setting. I have found that the best way to gather the equipment you need is to write

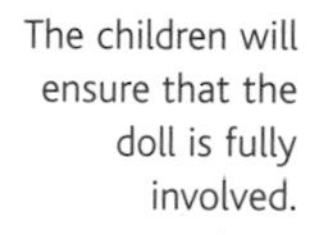

The children will ensure that the doll is fully involved.

out a shopping list and then show it to parents asking if they have any items stashed in their attic or garage. It is amazing what turns up and you may find a grandparent offering to readjust a nursery sweatshirt to fit the doll or a complete wardrobe. It is also a great way of getting parents involved from the start.

What happens if one child doesn't want anyone else to have contact with the doll?

I have heard of this happening occasionally and I am inclined to ask practitioners when they raise this concern if there is actually anything wrong with one child spending extra time with the doll if they are gaining some emotional comfort or support from it. I cannot stress enough that in situations like this you must look at the individual child's needs. I would suggest that working closely with the parents on any strategy involving the doll will benefit the child rather than simply removing the doll from the child without consultation.

Here is how one setting came up with a useful way of trying to avoid this situation arising in the first place. They created a special card tag which looked rather like the door hangers you are given in hotels to tell the cleaners to leave you in peace. The staff had put a photograph of the doll on the hanger and clearly marked it with the doll's name. Each morning the hanger was placed onto a different child's coat peg and when they came in they knew that whoever's peg it was on was the dolls 'special friend' for the day. If the child chose not to be with the doll at any point they were able to

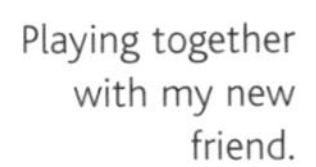

Playing together with my new friend.

Any doll can become an Empathy Doll.

relinquish this role and allow another child to take over. This method appeared to prevent any one child from monopolising the doll. It also gave staff a chance to encourage specific children to spend time with the doll if they felt the child would particularly benefit from the experience, for instance, if they were going through a time of particular stress or emotional upheaval.

Do you need more than one doll in a setting?

Experience has shown that in most cases there comes a point when to benefit all children in your setting you will need more than one Empathy Doll. This is for a number of reasons and is dependent upon the way your setting is structured and of course on monetary constraints.

As discussed when looking at how to develop your doll's story, you should not load all manner of social and emotional issues onto just one doll. So to be able to cover the range of experiences of the children in your setting you may find that you need more than one doll.

As well as maintaining a balance of doll stories reflective of every child you will need to consider the age of the dolls. As the Empathy Dolls Approach asks that the doll travels through the setting with children of a similar age to itself there may come a time when a doll moves to a different room, and you will need to establish a new doll in its place. The idea is that as the doll reaches a point where it moves onto the next setting it can be

When children do messy play, Empathy dolls do messy play!

stripped down and reinvented as someone new for use in the youngest age group. This develops an ongoing, rolling programme of dolls and could be used just in the nursery or foundation unit or could be extended throughout a whole primary school. I know of schools where there is a doll in every class from nursery to Year 6.

This rolling approach does not work so easily in preschool settings with mixed age groups or in childminder settings where children vary in age and may stay in the care of the same individual for many years.

In preschool settings or foundation rooms where there are mixed age groups I would suggest introducing more then one doll quite quickly to span the ages. You could also try keeping a doll to one side so that when a doll leaves the setting to move to pastures new you can introduce the new doll in at the earliest age group. This would avoid any confusion that might arise if you just reinvented the doll that left, as some children would already be accustomed to it in its previous guise.

In childminder settings I always advocate getting together with other practitioners to develop your doll's stories. Not only does this allow you access to a wider range of issues and characteristics not necessarily affecting your own Empathy Doll but you also have the option to swap dolls before reinventing their stories. This is a useful way to share resources when trying to provide high quality access to EYFS on the limited budget of a childminder.

Case study

I once trained a husband and wife childminder team in how to use the Empathy Dolls Approach at a point quite early on in their joint childcare careers. They both embraced the approach wholeheartedly and the children benefited enormously from their interactions with the dolls. One day some months after their initial training the couple contacted me to say that they had an issue that they could not resolve between them. They attended another training session I was running locally and put the dilemma to the rest of the group in the hope of finding a suitable solution.

The dilemma: When they had started with the approach the couple were caring for only a few children. Their success and growing confidence in recent months led to them taking on more children. They were now up to their legal limit of 7 children (9 including their two dolls!). Their problem was they only had a vehicle with 7 seats and so there was no longer a safe car seat for either of their dolls.
The solution: The dolls both developed travel sickness and now have to walk to wherever the children are going, meeting them at their destination without the need for a new car or breaking the law on car seats! They are actually surreptitiously pulled out of rucksacks upon arrival hopefully before the children notice!

Solutions to most problems can be found with a little bit of creative thinking using your personal knowledge of the children in your care. Be flexible, be sensitive, be creative.

8 Using Empathy Dolls to build home/school links

'Parents are children's first and most enduring educators. When parents and practitioners work together in early years settings, the results have a positive impact on children's development and learning' *DCSF 2008*

When developing the Empathy Dolls Approach I was very keen that the scope of the dolls should extend beyond the early years settings and into the home. My experience in early years and special school settings highlighted the importance of working in partnership with parents and carers. It is vital to ensure that any approach aimed at supporting children's emotional development is part of their whole life experience and not just limited to inside the school buildings. As someone who welcomes parents with open arms into the classroom I know only too well what a valuable, supportive resource they can be and how much most parents are desperate to feel a part of their child's life at your setting. Most parents I have met yearn to be a part of their child's learning beyond collecting junk modelling materials and buying the obligatory summer fête raffle tickets. The need for positive partnerships with parents has recently been highlighted in the new Early Years Foundation Stage document (DCSF 2008).

Sending Empathy Dolls home

After the dolls have been firmly established within the setting the possibility of letting them go home for 'sleepovers' arises. This can achieve a number of different things when done with some prior thought and planning. Experience has shown that using the Empathy Dolls Approach can act as an excellent stepping stone on which to build positive links between home and settings. I often get practitioners contacting me to say that they have been struggling to build a rapport with a particular set of parents or carers and that sending the doll home has given them the perfect opportunity to begin the communication process. It seems to provide a safe, comfortable starting point for parents and carers to share with staff their experiences and begin discussions. It acts as the ice-breaker that many practitioners are often searching for.

One childminder's account below shows how effective the approach can be in helping to support children's development within the home as well as building home-setting links.

This is an excellent example of a young child finding and displaying empathy. I have kept in touch with this childminder and I know that Simon has continued to be a regular visitor at James' house and has proved a great support to both him and his family!

Another setting contacted me to say how one of their dolls had helped a child become less distressed when out shopping with her mum. After mum had gotten over the initial embarrassment of pushing a child-sized doll around and talking to it as well as her daughter, she realised that the doll's presence had a strangely calming effect on the child who had previously screamed all the way round the shop. In hindsight I'm not sure who the doll had helped the most? The daughter, who had a focus for her attentions as she was pushed backwards around the endless aisles of boring cans and bottles (a design fault in shopping trolleys)? Or the mother who was helped to make positive conversations with her daughter and this ultimate distraction technique resulting in a calmer, less stressed parent and a much more relaxing shopping experience?

Case study

One day James's mum came to me in desperation. She said she was at the end of her tether and couldn't think what else to do. Her son had, over recent weeks, developed a reluctance to accept that anyone else was able to win at any activity he was taking part in. It had resulted in tantrums when he didn't win at sports day, or wasn't the proud recipient of the first prize in the cub scout's raffle and he was absolutely distraught and inconsolable when losing at board games within the setting.

In a bid to help I suggested that our Empathy Doll Simon went for a sleepover with James and his family as he was not feeling very happy and he could do with some cheering up. James jumped at the chance to have this well-loved member of our group come home with him and his mum said she was willing to try anything. Although she did add, 'There's no way this is going to work, but what have we got to lose?'

I thought little of it again until the phone rang at 10.30pm that night. I answered to find a delighted and yet surprised mum on the other end! 'We've been playing every game we can find in the house, and even some we have made up, and Simon has won nearly all of them'. She related how she had sat down and discussed with James how the doll might be feeling and how they might be able to cheer him up. She was then astonished to see that James readily accepted Simon winning games as he realised it would probably make Simon feel better!

About your new visitor......

Dear Parents,

Thank you for letting Charlie stay over night with your family. He has brought his pyjamas, his hairbrush and his toothbrush. Please make sure he brushes his teeth before bedtime.

Charlie will really enjoy joining in with everything you and your child do while he is staying with you. He likes to let the other children know what he gets up to when he stays at someone's house and so he has brought his camera to photograph your adventures.

Charlie has also brought with him a fun activity which he would like to share with you and your child.

We hope you all have loads of fun!!!!

From all the staff and children at Early Ideas Nursery School

Always send home an explanatary letter when a doll goes to stay.

In sending the dolls home you can also help to build up the parent's appreciation of the need for play-based learning. Even in these days of Early Years Foundation Stage where play-based learning is hailed as best practice, some parents struggle to see what their child can learn from playing with toys.

General guidelines for sending dolls home are:

- Do not send any doll home until the approach is firmly established within your setting and parents are used to seeing the doll involved with their children's activities. This tends to ensure that peer pressure from other parents and children ensure that the doll returns to the setting. I know of Empathy Dolls being used in some of the most 'challenging' areas in the UK and have never heard of a doll not coming back.
- Make sure you let parents know about the Empathy Dolls Approach before sending a doll home either via a face to face meeting, parents workshop or a letter similar to the one shown above.
- Make sure that the dates when the doll is visiting each child can be clearly seen by all. This not only reassures children that they will each get a turn but allows parents the opportunity to plan what they are going to do when it is their turn. Parents do have a tendency to get as enthusiastic as the children about the visit and I have known dolls visit parks, sea life centres, stately homes, tourist attractions and even go on holiday with families. One doll was even given her own seat on the aeroplane by a particularly sympathetic cabin crew member (I have seen the pictures!).

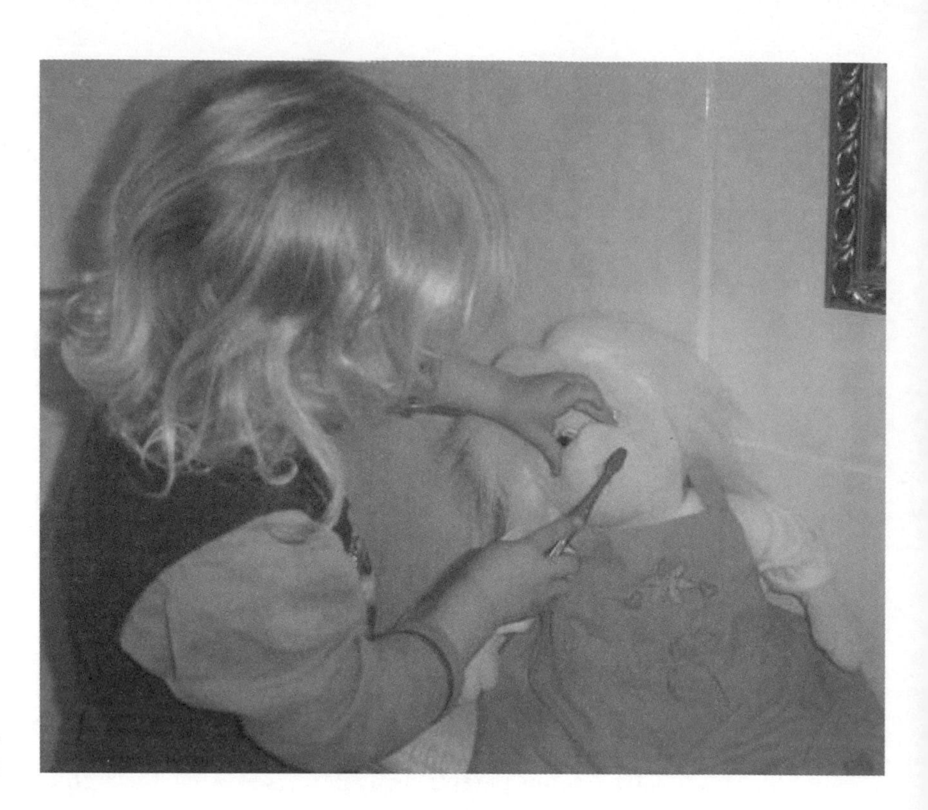

Don't forget your toothbrush!

- Make sure the doll has an overnight bag containing all the things a child would need on an overnight stay including pyjamas, slippers, toothpaste, toothbrush, cuddly toy, etc. A picture list is a good idea to make sure everything comes back and is a fantastic matching activity for the parent and child to complete together. Include a throw away camera in your overnight bag so the parents can record all of the exciting adventures the children have had with your doll.

9 Using Empathy Dolls as starting points for everyday situations

In this final section of the book I will consider a number of everyday situations experienced by children and begin to discuss ways in which your doll could be used as a tool to help build emotional awareness in your setting. The Empathy Dolls approach is far from being a complete solution; it needs to be used as part of a much wider approach to developing emotional awareness on a daily basis. For this reason I have also tried to include some suggestions for activities I have come across over the years which could be used to help children build coping strategies when dealing with these everyday situations. Hopefully by this point you will be viewing everyday activities through a child's eyes and the possibilities for support and continued care will be endless.

Dolls can be used with groups, pairs and individual children.

Using dolls to support the development of emotional awareness

There are three main ways in which the dolls can be used to highlight emotional issues and to support children in settings. An example of each approach follows but should not be viewed as the definitive guidance for using your doll. You know the children in your care and you can use this powerful tool to help children in many other ways. If one day just having a cuddle with the doll will comfort one particular child, it may prove more powerful than any planned discussion or activity.

The doll that has already experienced a situation

In this instance the doll has already experienced the situation or activity in question and through discussion can help to reassure the children. It is important for children to know that other people experience similar feelings and emotions when faced with a particular situation.

Example – Going on holiday

I have chosen this as an example because it provides scope to explore a number of other relevant issues as part of the discussion. In this scenario the doll has already been on holiday and over a period of two weeks has sent a number of postcards back to the setting to show children where he has been. Upon returning to the setting the doll is able to show the children a wide range of photographs of him at various different stages of his holiday including the airport, on the aeroplane, at the hotel, at the beach, at the shops, etc. This encourages children to share and talk about feelings and emotions evoked at all stages of the holiday.

As adults we are often guilty of only discussing the excitement and positive feelings associated with going on holiday. Rarely do I see opportunity given to discussing any potential worries or anxieties that may be arising in the run up to the holidays. As practitioners working with children, and particularly working with the Empathy Dolls Approach, we should be thinking more from the child's perspective and identifying a whole range of feelings both positive and negative. We must give children the confidence to speak up if they do not feel the same as the child next to them about the situation in question.

When thinking about holidays we should acknowledge that as well as feeling excited and happy some children could also potentially be feeling one or more of the following:

- **Fear** – of the airport, of flying, of going somewhere strange, that things will not be the same when they get back

- **Anxiety and nervousness** – about new unknown situations, that the food might be different, and generally not knowing what to expect
- **Worry** – at leaving behind family and friends, will they be there when I get back, will they still be my friend when I get back?
- **Stressed** – sometimes we build up the hype around going on holiday so that the whole experience can prove quite stressful for a child especially when parents start to stress about packing, travelling, money, etc.

The following scenario highlights the fact that we as adults can be guilty of trying to impose on children how we think they 'should' feel in a particular situation, instead of actually taking time to listen. Children often don't see the world the same way as we do and provision needs to be made so that everyone's feelings are valued and acknowledged.

Case study

Not quite the perfect surprise!

One parent recalled how she had spent weeks planning a much needed break away with her child. She had decided that as the child loved aeroplanes and everything to do with airports it would be a great idea to keep the planning for the holiday secret, aiming to surprise the child with a trip on an aeroplane, but it didn't quite go to plan!

When they finally arrived at the airport, instead of being elated at the thought of going on the aeroplane the child started to cry uncontrollably. A shocked and stunned mum took quite some time to calm the child and finally establish the root of the child's distress. He took a deep breath, looked his mother in the eye and said with an air of utter disappointment, 'You lied to me mummy!'

A lesson in how much her child truly used her as the measure of truthfulness and all that was good – that was his perspective on the world!

Supporting the child in your setting

There are many resources and activities you could set up to help the children work through any issues arising from holidays. Many practitioners would offer to set up a travel agent role-play area in the summer term. My concern with this comes from the reasons behind the setting up of such an area. Is it to help the children develop their imaginative play? Or is it because we want it to reflect the child's own life experiences and help them to build their understanding of real-life situations? I would hope the answer would be the latter but then we could ask, 'How real is a travel agent to a child of this age in 2009?'. With the rise of the internet less of us venture onto the high street in search of a bargain break, and how many would choose to go accompanied by an active and inquisitive toddler or preschooler?

A little more thought about the way that situations during holidays can affect children leads quickly to an alternative fun, and exciting role-play experience which is within the personal experiences of the children you are trying to engage and support – an airport!

As well as role-play situations, other suggestions for supporting children going on holiday include:

- Make available all year round a wide range of fiction and non-fiction books about all aspects of holidays
- Create airports, beaches, hotels, etc. in miniature for use during floor-play activities
- Set up a beach for the outdoor learning environment and let the doll wear his swimming costume
- Look at posters, pictures and postcards from other people's holidays
- Make a picture timeline of your doll's holiday

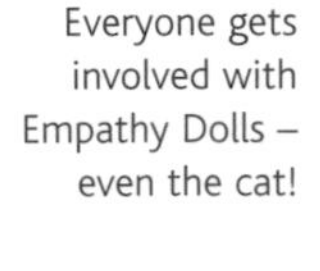

Everyone gets involved with Empathy Dolls – even the cat!

The doll that is about to experience something

This time the doll becomes the focus for discussion about a situation that they have yet to experience. They wish to share their feelings, hopes and/or anxieties about this with the children who subsequently take on the role of reassuring the doll. It is good for children to take on this role and to have opportunities to share their own experiences and feelings in support of another. It also helps to build the child's understanding that other people do experience the same and similar situations to themselves – a key factor in building empathy, self-esteem and self-confidence.

Example – Having a new baby in the family

This situation is a huge event in any child's life and can be seen as a 'triple whammy' on the emotional front for a small child. It brings with it a wave of emotions in three separate stages: before the birth, when the baby arrives, and a few months after the birth.

Before the birth

For many children there is excitement and happiness at the prospect of a new baby brother or sister, the chance to share life's experiences with a sibling. However, sometimes there can also be uncertainty about what it all means, anxiety over the unknown and what actually is in mummy's tummy? At the same time, mum may be getting more and more tired and less able to play with the child as she may have been able to before. This can sometimes lead to frustration and resentment, coupled with concern for the mother.

When the baby arrives

This is the immediate days and weeks after the birth when the focus is firmly on the new arrival and mum. This is a period of massive adjustment for the older sibling in which some children will experience feelings such as jealousy, frustration and even resentment, where as others enjoy every second of the new baby and revel in everyone making a fuss of them as well as the baby.

Some months after the birth

As early years practitioners we should also consider children's feelings some months after the happy event when the new baby can often start to impact directly on the young child's immediate experience and routines. Recent health recommendations state that babies should sleep in the same room as their parents for the first six months before moving to a cot in their own room. It is then that the older child often finds themselves sharing their private space with a new individual

Helping our friends when they most need us.

and experiencing the joy of sleepless nights. Then come the mixed emotions and feelings relating to sharing your possessions as the baby gets older.

The Empathy Doll can talk about all three stages of the new baby's arrival and help the children to prepare for this life-changing experience.

Supporting the child in your setting

Don't just stick to the traditional role-play scenarios such as a baby clinic or hospital.

Nowadays many mums are home within days if not hours after giving birth and so the hospital environment is not always a relevant real-life situation. The parents may utilise the childcare you provide as an opportunity to visit the baby clinic with one less little person to keep an eye on. Yet in the run up to a baby arriving most children will visit a number of well-known baby superstores on a number of occasions and a role-play area which reflects this can provide access to all the paraphernalia that comes with the new baby and also places the role-play firmly within the child's direct scope of reference. After the birth a home corner with additional cot, baby bath, buggy and toys can help children to live out the experiences and issues they are having in their own home lives.

As well as role-play there are many other things you could do in your setting to explore the issue of a new baby arriving including a display of adults and children from the nursery as babies. The children will realise that we were all babies once. Also, of course, make a collection of fiction and non-fiction books on the subject to encourage children to talk about their feelings with you and the Empathy Doll.

The doll that experiences things alongside the children – a shared experience

In this third example the doll experiences the situation alongside the children. This joint experience allows the child to feel supported at every step by the doll's presence and the shared aspect serves to build on the bond between the child and the doll, making the doll even more of a powerful tool over time.

Example – Toilet training

When looking to use the dolls to support children as they undertake some of life's ongoing challenges this approach allows for continuous discussion and involvement. Dolls being used to help children as they master toilet training will have their own nappies, changes of clothes, potties, and will go with the children when they visit the toilet area. Seeing this process from a child's perspective will hopefully encourage staff to make the system of changing/toileting as stress free as possible and the toilet area a lot more pleasing to all of the children's senses. This is an excellent example of using verbal and non-verbal communication to express feelings. Remember just because children can't speak doesn't mean that they don't feel. You can build positive self-esteem in even the very youngest of babies by this method.

Here are some other examples of situations where this 'buddy' system has been used effectively with Empathy Dolls:

- Helping a child through transition from one setting to another
- Helping a child separate from a parent or carer at the beginning of the day
- Learning to dress themselves
- Developing mealtime skills

Whatever your chosen method of using the dolls in your setting make sure that you always take the time to see the world from the child's perspective and allow everyone to have their own feelings in any one situation. Most of all listen properly to what the child is trying to tell you and acknowledge their feelings however irrational they may seem to you!

The first duty of love is to listen

When I ask you to listen to me, and you give me advice,
You have not heard what I asked of you.
When I ask you to listen and you tell me why I shouldn't feel as I do,
You are trampling on my feelings.
When I ask you to listen and you feel you have to find solutions to my problems,
I feel let down… strange as it may seem!

Please listen.

All I ask is that you listen.

Not talk, or do, or advise…

JUST LISTEN.

Advice is cheap, I can get that anywhere.
I can do for myself, I am not helpless.
Maybe discouraged and faltering, but not helpless.

When you do something for me that I can and need to do for myself,
You contribute to my fear and reinforce my weaknesses.

When you accept as a simple fact, that I feel what I feel,
(However irrational it may seem to you),
Then I can quit trying to convince you and I can explore this, that irrational feeling.
When that is clear, the answers are obvious and I don't need advice.

My irrational fears make sense when I can discover what is behind them.

If you listen, and understand, I can work things out for myself.

So I ask again, just listen.

And if you too have something to say… be patient,

Then I will listen to you.

Source Unknown – cited in (Dent. M 2005)

Conclusion

I have now given you the basic tools for implementing the Empathy Dolls Approach in your setting. I have presented the dos and don'ts and attempted to answer some of the most common questions. You, the practitioner are now hopefully beginning to see the importance of viewing the world through a child's eyes and coming to terms with how this can impact on your everyday practice. This is where the journey gets interesting. How this approach will take off in your setting, is up to you. Every setting has unique and wonderful children and staff and they will all work with this approach slightly differently. Stories of how the dolls help individual children in settings across the UK still fill me with a sense of awe at the creativity and commitment of the early years professionals involved. I look forward to hearing more!

However, what comes from this point on, is the opportunity to enhance the positive self-image and confidence of every child and adult you work with. Remember to let the children guide you through their world instead of trying to force your world on them and you will begin to experience what I believe is one of the best, most exciting and rewarding jobs there can be.

If I had my child to raise over again

by Diane Loomans

If I had my child to raise all over again,
I'd build self-esteem first, and the house later.
I'd fingerpaint more, and point the finger less.
I would do less correcting and more connecting.
I'd take my eyes off my watch, and watch with my eyes.
I would care to know less and know to care more.
I'd take more hikes and fly more kites.
I'd stop playing serious, and seriously play.
I would run through more fields and gaze at more stars.
I'd do more hugging and less tugging.
I'd see the oak tree in the acorn more often.
I would be firm less often, and affirm much more.
I'd model less about the love of power,
And more about the power of love.

References

Barnett. B, Dolby. R, Kelk. N, Lewin. V, Water. B & Ungerer. J.A. (1990) *The early development of empathy: Self-regulation and individual differences in the first year*

Motivation and Emotion Volume 14 No.2 pp 93–106 http://www.springerlink.com/content/g7t4288052132366

Brown. B. (2001) *Combating Discrimination – Persona Dolls in Action*; Trentham Books – Stoke on Trent

Calkins. S.D, & Gill. K.L. (2003) *Do aggressive/destructive toddlers lack concern for others? Behavioral and physiological indicators of empathic responding in 2-year-old children* Development and Psychopathology, 15 , pp 55–71

Carr. L, Dubeau. M.C, Lacoboni. M, Lenzi. G.L. & Mazziotta. J.C. (2003) *Neural mechanisms of empathy in humans: A relay from neural systems for imitation to limbic areas*; PNAS (Proceedings of the National Academy of Sciences of the United States of America) Volume 100 No.9 pp 5497–5502

Coplan R.J, Girardi. A, Findlay. L.C. (2006) *Links between empathy, social behaviour and social understanding in early childhood*; Early Childhood Research Quarterly, Volume 21 Issue 3 pp 347–359

Dent. M. (2005) *Nurturing Kids Hearts and Souls – Building Emotional, Social and Spiritual Competency*; Pennington Publications, Dunsborough

DfES (2004) *Every Child Matters – Change for Children*

Goleman. D. (1996) *Emotional Intelligence – Why it can matter more than IQ*; Bloomsbury, London

Hinnant. J.B & O'Brien M. (2007) *Cognitive and emotional control and perspective taking and their relations to empathy in 5-year-old children*; Journal of Genetic Psychology Volume 168 No.3 pp 301–322

Hamazaki. T. (1992) *Preschool children's prosocial judgments and their reasoning in the empathic situations* Shinrigaku Kenkyu. (The Japanese Journal of Psychology) Volume 62 No.6 pp 364–368

Hoffman M.L. (2000) *Empathy and Moral Development*; Cambridge University Press, New York

Loomans, Diane (1994, 2003) *100 Ways to Build Self-Esteem and Teach Values*, HJ Kramer/New World Library, CA.

Maslow A.H. (1943) *A Theory of Human Motivation*; Psychological Review, Volume 50, pp 370–396

'In a sorry state of mind – Were the motorists who drove past Cait Atkins lacking in empathy? Science has the answer.' Article by Kate Wighton June 10 2006 http://www.timesonline.co.uk/tol/news/uk/health/article672972.ece

Additional Information

Dolls which can be used to support this approach can be purchased from many companies including:

www.playmerrily.co.uk
www.ascoeducational.co.uk
www.puppetsbypost.co.uk